Praise for Jeremy Ra's *Another Way of Loving Death*

"These exquisite poems explore the poet's history and humanity. Steeped in revery, layered with longing, surrealism nudges up against erotica and memory, and the result, often devastating, is nothing less than brilliant."

— Alexis Rhone Fancher, author of *Junkie Wife*

Praise for Aruni Wijesinghe's *2 Revere Place*

"I can't remember being so easily persuaded, so hypnotized by a cycle of poems. This is a splendid book, at once sober and fantastic, morally acute and unpretentious. Trust this poet."

— Brendan Constantine, author of *Dementia, My Darling*

GOD IS A RIVER RUNNING DOWN MY PALM

pictureshowpress.net

Cover Image Credit: Arelix, depositphotos
Author Image(s) Credit: Alexis Rhone Fancher

FIRST EDITION

ISBN-13: 979-8-9850690-6-8

God is a river running down my palm

Jeremy Ra & Aruni Wijesinghe

PICTURE SHOW PRESS

POEMS

FROM THE EDITOR

In 2019, I put out a call on Facebook asking if any poets I knew would be interested in writing a duet chapbook that explored the concepts of the female (and male) gaze. I think at the time I was inspired by Chris Kraus' *I Love Dick* (as well as the TV series).

The female gaze is certainly not a new concept and wasn't exactly new to me then, either—years ago, I must have watched fifteen or so seasons of *America's Next Top Model* (a guilty pleasure if there ever was one), and one of the photo challenges involved each model posing for a women's magazine and then for a men's magazine, during the same photoshoot, wearing the same bathing suit.

Fast forward to 2024 and the collaboration you now hold in your hands has long since transcended the concepts of the male and female gazes—it is now centered around what is at the focal point of any poet's gaze: desire.

This is beyond fitting because, if I'm being totally honest with myself, I was really posting the literary equivalent of a *thirst trap* when I put out that initial call, meaning I wholeheartedly intended that post to capture the interest of one specific person. (It did, by the way, but the point is that poetry saw right through my pretenses, shed the trappings of the "original" concept, and decided on desire.)

Throughout these poems, desire flashes us all its gorgeous, devastating angles—of course there are longing poems and horny poems and hungry poems ("in still life I can't help but see / a nude female body," "our open mouths bold enough to eat," "the world won't hear us, but the night / remembers this breath"), but there are also poems pining for the past, pining for health, pining for the ability (and the freedom) *to* pine ("If the cage I'm trapped in is desire / or its absence, I want to want again").

In her novel *Their Eyes Were Watching God*, author Zora Neale Hurston writes, "There are years that ask and years that answer." Well, there are also poems that ask and poems that answer, and both can be found in the book you're holding. And so now, a proposition: Desire is beckoning. Do you follow?

Shannon
Picture Show Press

On Las Ramblas, You Stop to Take a Photo

after Jo Knoblock Castillo's Blue Window

We plant red geraniums
outside my window, blue sills
beaching in the noonday bright,

but this is not Spain. We buy
terra cotta pots on sale
at the local garden center, turn

chipped lips towards the wall.
We salvage curtains from Goodwill,
steep lace in the bathroom sink,

scrub out years. We whitewash
the house, but the dust still settles
into the stucco, marking the time

since you last said you imagine me
my younger self. Us backpacking
through Europe. Remember the way

I'd shield my eyes from Barcelona suns,
framed in a viewfinder? I am still that girl
on the platform, choosing tomorrow

from the train schedule, destinations
scrolling down the wall, a girl in love
with fate's rolled dice.

— *Aruni Wijesinghe*

Eyes Full of Moon

after Joni Mitchell

Richard, nothing's been the same since last
we spoke, yet nothing has changed.

I didn't want to tell you I arranged trips to two more cities,
just so my visit to you

wouldn't stand out in your mind.
No pressure, I had said. *This is just another stop.*

I never was good at lying.
I digest time in morsels.

I went to Prague before our date in Vienna.
I had lunch in front of a castle,

drank wine on a boat. I wanted to be a film
before I met up with you.

That night, I kept walking
the cobblestoned streets—all the red lights

seemed intent on speaking.
Do you know what I envy

about the moon?
That it can fade to nothing

yet get full again.
I still love the syrupy taste

of a good lie.
How much strength

does one need
to nurture a remembrance?

At the café where I met you,
you picked up a cigarette, each puff

you blew cratered my eyes.
How I couldn't stop staring

at your hands as we walked
through the Innere Stadt.

What we didn't say that day
is why glass beads are frozen

on the moon.

— *Jeremy Ra*

we slip on a dark skin of words

incarnate histories
bridge continents
climb the stairs
of high rise apartment buildings

leave the clamor of America on the doormat
remove our shoes, walk gentle into the house
build a home enough
for ancestors and children
to sit together

pass the rice and dhal,
eat with fingertips stained turmeric,
smell of cardamom clinging to our hair

we mingle English and Sinhala
our open mouths bold enough to eat
two worlds at once

— *Aruni Wijesinghe*

Thaaththi poses like *The Dying Gaul*

in the garden at Versailles. He stretches out
in front of the marble reproduction,
stifles a smile. He mimics
a dying hero, semi-reclined
on the crushed stone path.

Ammi will label this overcast day in France,
her precise handwriting cataloging
perfection. A satin Kodak moment
tucked into a pocket of the family album.
Thaaththi, a young god
in maroon windbreaker
and bell-bottomed jeans.

Malli stands behind *Thaaththi*,
his tiny body pressed to a block of stone.
A study in concentration, his eyes
never leaving his fallen hero. A moment after
the photo is snapped, he rushes
to *Thaaththi's* side, checks him
for invisible wounds.

Ammi's eye composes the moment,
what a father can teach a son,
the glorious beauty of decay.

— *Aruni Wijesinghe*

Barley Hill

after Aruni Wijesinghe's "we slip on a dark skin of words"

And if you managed to climb the hill,
the barley meant a gift of another year,

so you savored every last bite of it.
The grains needed to be scorched,

cooked in a metal pot prone to overheat.
The burnt part preserved for darker days.

What's burnt is a mistake.
What's a mistake endures.

Despite my grandfather claiming noble origins,
what I have is a peasant's ingenuity.

How else would I have known to spread
my minimum being into so many nights

by the precipice of being out on the street?
Behind every glutton is a pauper.

Whetted in days when
a meal was a bucket of water, the sigh

is what cut the shepherd's purse
rustling in a bed of soy.

The clear broth soaking the grain
dirties like the color of pine bark

stripped to be eaten.
No, it's not that I remember—

it's that I cannot forget.
This barley, this steaming,

unreasonable need to live.
All the blood shed for the feast.

— Jeremy Ra

After the Korean War, in South Korea, "barley hill" meant a critical period in late spring when rice harvested the previous autumn had run out but the spring barley was not yet harvested.

(Description borrowed and modified from Tae-Ho Kim, *The Good, the Bad, and the Foreign: Trajectories of Three Grains in Modern South Korea.*)

Bobbin Winding

after Oswaldo Guayasamín's Manos insaciables

I skip the step where I spindle
the main thread onto the machine.
I engage the winder, press the ball
of my foot against the treadle.

The spool whizzes and skips
in my cupped hand. Blue cotton cuts
a hot line across flesh, stitches
a new road into the map of my palm.

This is how time passes, a thread
singing from spool to bobbin,
carving the space between now
and yet-to-come.

— *Aruni Wijesinghe*

Stilled Life

after Paul Cézanne's Still-Life with a Watermelon and Pomegranates

I'll take a pair of pomegranates
and return you two ruddy breasts,
see your battered wooden table
and raise you Versailles' ballroom floor

in still life I can't help but see
a nude female body, collection of limbs
of an overripe odalisque
insouciant, lolling on a bench

I trade domesticity for panoramas
wander a medina of cobalt glass
porcelain tureen turned distant minaret
call of the muezzin high above the din

replace a melon's blue rind
with an oblong globe, stretched taut
let me spill a universe of red pith
quick, hand me a knifepoint

— *Aruni Wijesinghe*

Twelve Suns

The next day she finds
the box amongst the cards,
gift bags and bottles of wine.
She lifts the lid, discovers
a dozen *kesar pedas*,
each a perfect daisy.

She raises a gold flower
to her lips. The sweet
dissolves into her.
She swallows
a crumbling sun.

— *Aruni Wijesinghe*

I Got Lost and Ended Up Posing as a Watermelon in His Painting

after Paul Cézanne's Still-Life with a Watermelon and Pomegranates

I pose for him with all my glee,
because that's what I was told
would attract attention.

I polish my impregnable, big rind—
my shame-averse skin that even hippos
need an iron jaw to break.

When I crack a smile,
it is chiseled.

I am not easily bent on whims or sins.
Yes, you could almost say I'm happy—

happy enough to grow in my oblong shape
like that of a tear that cannot drop.

But when I see myself painted
through his digging eyes, I am blue—
many, heavy shades of blue.

Less a balloon than a dire drag
that rings in the nether region's decibel
like drums or bass.

I grow heavier on the page with each stroke.

I pose for him still,
letting my rinds go slightly bestial,
slightly dull.

I spread like an ever-dipping
web that nets the coarser pains.
His eyes rope cinder blocks

around my ankles for we have stared
each other down into the ripples
of nothing upon nothing upon nothing.

If I had a mouth,
I would marry my grief
to his.

— Jeremy Ra

I Am Staring at a Boy Tanning on the Chaise Lounge

and I fixate on him like he's some model
in an underwear ad I saw in the very first copy
of *Rolling Stone* I ever held in my hands.
(Or was it *LA Xpress*?)

The desire is so thick, it muffles me
like propaganda, and just feeling this
is good enough to be real.
Knowing he's wising up

to my flatlined stare
doesn't make me turn away.
He adjusts himself
as if to give a better sideview.

Then I think about what it takes
for two people to come together
when we're fed so many angels
and no wings. We've coined awful

terms for acceptance—like *compromise,*
sacrifice—and I could love all
or none when love, with its instrument,
is not a harp but a scalpel,

others a self from me.
His glances thrown my way
X-ray me skeletal. Shall I buy him a drink?
Would I swim toward him to show him

my hands that were incubated in the breath
of small losses? Gathering water, I'd say:
no pressure, these hands know how to hold on
as much as how to let go.

The sun, half-mooned to the fringe,
spills its last shift into the pool.
For the life we do not share, I will not grieve.
Watch the ripples steady.

All that will not happen has happened.

— Jeremy Ra

On Imagining Porn That Is Not There

after Jo Knoblock Castillo's Blue Window

If it's in focus, it's pornography, if it's out of focus, it's art.
— Billy Kwan, *"The Year of Living Dangerously"*

We walk the Louvre, ignore penises
as if such exposure were incidental—
and all of us nod *Art*,
while making sure our gazes
do not linger too long at certain angles.

We imagine the hands
that had to chisel the marble
only to come up short
of the white-hot of the flesh—
imagine fingernails at rest,
too stucco to hold a member.

If someone were to ask me what art is good for,
I would say: *capturing the naked.*

In this one painting, the curtains are drawn
against a pot of cardinal geraniums.
I think I've seen such hush in porn—

the nineties porn where you'd have to pull back
dingy velvet curtains to embrace the peepshow
of an "Adults Only" section—
torsos and buttocks enlarged,
asking *but aren't these just body parts?*

But they were not.

My temperature would rise
among the oily, sleek porn covers
set in places like St. Tropez—

shiny men on a boat,
their erections, a crash course in sailing.
Their grinding chests and groins,
the means to spark another fatal fire
under the sun.

Or waxed men in their prime
lounging in front of a villa,
where not a hair, not a red flower
behind the ears of their nude bodies
was out of place.

I miss the thoughtfulness in porn.

In *Sympathy for Lady Vengeance*,
the heroine's weapon of choice
is an ornate handgun with a short,
impractical range.

*Because everything needs
to be beautiful.* And close.
Even bloodshed.

Even geraniums, potted like jewels
in front of the movie set's curtains
with their lips shut.

Some hands must have probed
the dirt to perfect such a bloody blossom.

My gaze fumbles toward art
to ensnare all the naked men.

— *Jeremy Ra*

Killing Time

another inky Friday in L.A. and we're clothed
in midnight and old concert t-shirts
after a long night of Genuine Drafts
last slices of Domino's long gone cold

meditation in a darkened den
with nothing to light the night
but the glow of stereo components
and the bulb above the kitchen stove

Dark Side of the Moon revolves
the forty-three-minute cycle a grudge match
of who would bark shins on the coffee table,
press the winking CD *Play* button again

our only conversation an incredulous
fuck, this is a great album
followed by boozy laughter, shifting
of Styrofoam pellets in bean bag chairs

like the murmur of a vast ocean, tipping
the balance of our collective consciousness
drifting kelp of pre-dawn philosophies
waving in the amniotic night

an endless current of small hours,
we stay up all night, this scene on repeat
variation of beers and albums inconsequential
time irrelevant against our immortality

Jeff, Ron and I cocooned in our truth
of friendship unchanged, ever young
as the bright face of the moon rising
over Blockbuster Video on Wilshire

— *Aruni Wijesinghe*

Boys Sleeping

Running into you in the school bathroom
underlines me like a book title.
I synopsize excuses you'd make

to stand closer. We walk home seemingly
together, stumble into booths
where we spend more than our allowances

on sticker pictures that we paste
to the back of our hidden diaries
with Sanrio stationery. I see my veins glow

in a way they shouldn't. We don't slip
notes to each other in classes, but somehow
find a way to walk home together, blended

with other boys in the same uniforms.
At our friend's house, whose parents
are away, we watch a porno. I wonder

if anyone notices our gazes
are elsewhere. Our story isn't here, even
in the disrobing of the primal.

Maybe we were created on the 8th day
because god installed cable TV
when he got tired of watching

the same old sex. Do you remember,
too, that once, flesh was mere wound,
the layer beneath the skin housing

a map of vessels? We invent a science
project we must work on that lets me
sleepover on a twin bed,

lights out, a quilt patterned
with little robots, your body heaves
next to mine—a running river, glistening,

noisy from the amphibians flailing
within. O rising croaks,
abduct us from the well we can't climb—

the world won't hear us, but the night
remembers this breath that shrouded
boys with the bluest veins.

— Jeremy Ra

Liang Zhu, or Butterfly Love

after Jeremy Ra's "Boys Sleeping"

When do we learn to be not ourselves?
As a child I would assume disguises, mask
my true desires. Beg for knowledge,
feign gender for a taste of more.
Boy's clothes were never enough costume
on the walk to school, pants I wore
to pursue first steps towards
my truer self. I created a face
to try on every morning, trained myself
to quiet my hungry heart in study hall.

Is education mere farce
learned on the journey into a world
beyond the laws of caste and class?
We bury our passion in books, swear
fraternal oaths, call it friendship.
How to still the pulse that threatens
to betray forbidden want?
Incense lingers on a wooden bridge,
whispers a truth you fail to notice.
Why turn a blind eye to burgeoning Spring,
call Mandarin ducks another ill-fated pair?

Is death defiance of expectation,
hurling myself into an open grave,
and love a pair of butterflies,
two ghosts reunited on the path
to the wedding banquet?

— *Aruni Wijesinghe*

The Ballad of Neurotransmittal Deficiency or An Ode to Wellbutrin

after Oswaldo Guayasamín's Manos insaciables

God is a river running down my palm—
the rising heat of cement sneaks up my back
like a creeping vine. In heated silence,
regret is a thing that mates with itself
and multiplies. I hear its buzz.
How fast and how far I imagine
I run into the streets that wind up away
from conspicuous breathing until I can look
down at an anguish that gets blurrier.
But blurry is a descriptor of a familiar thought—
the inevitable recognition still lies so bare,
it still rends my stomach to pieces.
I lose my touch, my hunger.

I have traced my palm and wondered
if the roads I tread were already carved—
if even the asking of why
is merely but a futile digging
to deepen a shallow range of variables
for a largely predictable outcome.
Then what about the thumbs-ups
and alohas, hallelujahs and namastes,
and all the incessant calling after god—
does knowing mean I will stop
pining? Or look at the past and its destruction
that narrow our boundaries of living.
If the cage I'm trapped in is desire
or its absence, I want to want again,
I want to be brokenly obsessed again
about nothing, about anything.

The cup I'm washing cracks in my hands.
I hold onto its sinking shards.
God, is a river running down my palm?

— *Jeremy Ra*

Madonna and Child

When the vertigo hits, the world won't stop
swimming. Furniture careens around the bedroom,
lamps melt sideways, pastel bedsheets undulate
in a lava field of percale flowers. I can't open
my eyes, can't keep the world pinned
in place without my body erupting in rivers
of piss and shit and puke.

My mother steadies a plastic trash bin
under my chin, coos endearments. She brushes
drool-wet hair back from my face, tells me
not to cry. I am fifty-three years old, post-op
from back surgery, and my Judas body
has launched another attack. I can't stop
weeping, can't stem the hysteria. She wipes snot
with the sleeve of her sweater, nonplussed.

She supports me during my stagger
to the bathroom, juggling my walker and trash bin.
An inch of vomit sloshes like an unholy tide.
I sob as she helps me out of my soiled nightshirt.
My cotton panties are stained beyond recovery.
In the cool of the shower she washes my hair
with lavender shampoo, combing out tangles.
She scrubs my back, careful to avoid my still-raw scar,
rinses the dread from my body. Never flinches
when I throw up again, just starts the process over.

While she swaddles me in terrycloth, I ask her
how she can stand it, this messy love. She says
I did this for you when you were an infant.
You're my baby. Nothing will ever change that.

— *Aruni Wijesinghe*

Dementia Asked If He Had a Son

Mother claims you have dementia,
and it feels like a cheap shot.

Your thoughts never started anywhere,
and never ended, like the clutches of an undertow.

You talked naturally demented your whole life.
(*Natural?* What does that even mean?)

When I loved a cartoon devil at six,
I asked you to draw his vengeance,

naked—the thing that made him
so sure of life—and without hesitation,

you gave me a pencil sketch
of the devil undressed.

This is what you see,
but do not believe in it.

You never did talk to me like a child—
a man who stood like a tower

I'd one day grow enough legs to scale,
a man who thought all men

should be feminists in the seventies.
You knew you couldn't lose when already lost.

Birthdays, matching shoes with belts,
even remembering the way back

from the grocery store doesn't excite you,
much to mother's chagrin. For only in losing

everything will pain relent—will find
and forget the devil within us, so cold.

So alive.

— Jeremy Ra

My Gal Mary

My steps would be heavy too
if a hundred gods clung to my back.
Each day a hundred heads scan
the traffic so mother wouldn't miss out
on the apocalypse.

Before my birth,
the dream god showed mother
I was a dragon
about to devour her—
but nothing else, beyond
the green, tendrilled jaw unhinging.

No one could show her the end she craved.
Not the pantry god. Not the shoe god.
But the number god, to cheer her up,
showed her a whip
with a spider-web snare to tame
the coming days.

She learned the numbers like penal codes,
and the stars sank each day
as misfortunes became destinies.
But it wasn't enough.
Never enough.

Mother acquired the Virgin Mary
along with her newest faith—
a porcelain statue as tall as a 2-year-old
with her arms always raised,
too awkwardly open
for any embrace
or carriage.

No one thought Mary would last,
but she learned to work with the other gods,
a machine of wish delegation.
All gods are wish-hearers,
but not granters.

They shoot the wishes
to the sky as best they can,
and all that miss the mark
form the droplets that torrent
back down to the earth.

Punctured by the hail
of my mother's granular wishes,
the lesser gods lost their efficacy
until all that was left standing
were the Buddha's meager protests.

Mary stayed serene
though being slighted was new to her.
The gods consoled her:

What chance did any of us have
if she could leave Siddhartha
after kneeling a thousand times
in a pool of blood?

Small consolation it turned out—
as mother took most of the gods with her
overseas, but not Mary,
who ended where I began.

I think about freeing Mary
from her porcelain frame
but lose heart—where else
except among my godless shelves,

can the ever-after's lonely flaw
repeat itself daily?

Behold: my pal Mary—
who knows I share her pulse
against my will,
who knows what it's like to bear
but a likeness
to what is really sought.

— *Jeremy Ra*

ACKNOWLEDGMENTS

Grateful acknowledgments to the following publications in which these poems first appeared:

2 Revere Place (Moon Tide Press, 2022): "we slip on a dark skin of words"

Another Way of Loving Death (Moon Tide Press, 2023): "Boys Sleeping"

ABOUT ARUNI

Aruni Wijesinghe lives and writes in Southern California, and can usually be found shelving books in the local public library. A project manager, ESL teacher, former sous chef and occasional belly dance instructor, she is a multiple Pushcart Prize and Best-of-the-Net nominee. Her work has been published in *Spillway*, *Cultural Daily*, *Redshift*, *a moon of one's own*, *The Journal of Radical Wonder*, and elsewhere.

She has multiple published collections including *2 Revere Place* (Moon Tide Press), *The Litany of Missing* and *Bedside Manners* (Arroyo Seco Press), and co-authored *The Undulating Line* (Picture Show Press). You can follow her on social media @aruniwrites (Instagram and Twitter) or on her website www.aruniwrites.com.

ABOUT JEREMY

Jeremy Ra is a queer, Chinese-Korean-American poet living in Los Angeles. A Best-of-the-Net and multiple Pushcart nominee, his poems have appeared in *Spillway*, *I-70 Review*, *Cultural Daily*, *San Diego Poetry Annual*, and *Catamaran Literary Reader*, among others. He was a twice-finalist for the Steve Kowit Poetry Prize and the recipient of the Morton Marcus Poetry Prize. His first chapbook, *Another Way of Loving Death*, was published by Moon Tide Press. He is a co-host of the video series, Poetry.la.

ABOUT PICTURE SHOW PRESS

Picture Show Press is a small press that publishes poetry chapbooks, novellas, and short story collections out of Southern California.

If you are a student in the U.S. and would like a free copy of any of the books in the Picture Show Press catalogue, please email pictureshowpress@gmail.com.

More Poetry Books from Picture Show Press

A sip of wind by Nora Simões
Alinea by Betsy Mars
Along the Fault Line by Tamara Madison
Between the Spine: A Collection of Erotic Love Poems
by Adrian Ernesto Cepeda
Concrete's Song by Lloyd David Aquino
daughter of salt by Chestina Craig
Girl On The Highway by Wendy Rainey
If your body is a broken landscape by Kathryn McMurray
Little Threats by Suzanne Allen
Quiver: A Sexploration by Holly Pelesky
Suddenly, All Hell Broke Loose!!! by Brian Harman
The Feather Ladder by Cindy Rinne
Witness: Selected Poems by George Hammons

www.ingramcontent.com/pod-product-compliance
Lightning Source LLC
Chambersburg PA
CBHW021147020426
42331CB00005B/942